MW01484963

How to Braid Hair

The Complete Guide to Braiding Hair in All the Most Popular Styles Today

Table of Contents

Introduction

I want to thank you and congratulate you for downloading the book "**How to Braid Hair**: *The Complete Guide to Braiding Hair in All the Most Popular Styles Today*".

This book contains proven steps and strategies on how to become truly beautiful and endearing by learning how to do different types of braids. Braiding is basically the act of intertwining or interweaving strands of hair. Aside from being one of the classic favorites when it comes to styling hair, braiding is also becoming popular again these days. Braided hair always elicits attention from people and that's why it would be good if you learn how to do it yourself. Perfect for everyday gatherings and even social occasions (such as parties and the like), braids will surely make you feel beautiful and confident.

Here's an inescapable fact: Braids are known to be the most ancient type of hairstyle. It has been around for over 30,000 years and was even used as a means of communication during the olden times. The hairstyle was also used to distinguish whether a woman is single or married. The kind of braid that a woman has was once considered a "mark", indicating whether she belong to a particular tribe.

Braiding is also a social art. In other words, because of the time they spend braiding, people begin to have some form of bond and start talking about their lives – sometimes, they even end up talking about whatever is going on in the world. Aside from that, when people watch you create braids, they will be tempted to learn how to do it too. That's why braiding is also considered as a means of socialization.

If you do not learn how to braid, you would be missing a lot because it means that you will have to hire someone else to style your hair, especially if there are events or parties that you have to attend. This would mean that you'll lose some money because you would have to pay those hairdressers, and these days, money really does not come easy and that's why you have to do whatever you can to make sure that you are able to save.

It's time for you to become your own hairstylist and learn how to do braids. It's fun, and you will not get bored because are there are many different kinds of braids that you can try. With the help of this book, you will learn to do almost all braiding techniques – from the simplest ones to the most extraordinary varieties. Now, you would have no problems about what to do with your hair when a special occasion comes up, or when you simply feel like fixing yourself up.

What are you waiting for? Start reading this book now and learn how to braid your hair quickly and easily.

Chapter 1: Simple Braids

Some easy-breezy, but nonetheless beautiful, braids that you'll be able to do in a minute or two!

Basic Braid

http://2good2lose.com/braids/basicbraid1.gif

Step 1: Tie your hair in a ponytail, and then separate it into three equal parts. Using your right hand, hold two strands with your palm (facing up). Afterwards, hold the third strand using your left hand.

http://2good2lose.com/braids/basicbraid2.gif

Step 2: With your palm facing down, turn your right hand over so that the strand on the right will now be in the middle and the middle strand will end up on the right side.

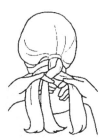

http://2good2lose.com/braids/basicbraid3.gif

Step 3: Now, switch hands and hold the strand on the right with your right hand and the left and middle strands with your left hand. Make sure that your left hand is facing up, and then turn it around so that it would shift to a facedown position.

Repeat steps 1 to 3 until you have finally braided all your hair. Once done, fasten everything together with an elastic band.

Knowing the most basic type of braiding will help you learn how to do other kinds, even the most complex ones.

The Rope Braid

http://2good2lose.com/braids/ropebraid1.gif

Step 1: Tie your hair in a ponytail, and then separate it into three strands. After doing that, use your left hand to hold two strands and hold one strand with your right hand.

http://2good2lose.com/braids/ropebraid2.gif

Step 2: Wind the strand that is in your right hand all around your right index finger, and then switch hands quickly so that all the strands will be in your right hand – only separated by your fingers. Hold the strands tightly to keep them in place.

http://2good2lose.com/braids/ropebraid3.gif

Step 3: Now, bring the wound strand over your hair so that it would end up on the left side. After, move all the strands back to your left hand.

http://2good2lose.com/braids/ropebraid4.gif

Step 4: Use your right hand to wind the right strand once more, and then repeat steps 2 to 3 until you have reached the end of the ponytail. Do not release until you have fastened it with an elastic, so that the rope would not unravel.

French Braid

http://2good2lose.com/braids/frenchbraid1.gif

Step 1: Take a section of hair from the top of your head, as seen on the image above, and separate it into 3 strands. Cross the strands left over middle, and then right over middle, just like how you'd do a basic braid.

http://2good2lose.com/braids/frenchbraid2.gif

Step 2: Now, use your left hand to hold all of the strands, but make sure that they are kept separate from one another.

http://2good2lose.com/braids/frenchbraid3.gif

Step 3: Gather a small section of hair from the right side of your head using your right hand, and then add it to the strand on the right.

http://2good2lose.com/braids/frenchbraid4.gif

Step 4: Bring the recently added strand to the middle, and then bring the strand in the middle to the right side.

http://2good2lose.com/braids/frenchbraid5.gif

Step 5: Switch hands and keep all strands separated, in order for your left hand to be free.

http://2good2lose.com/braids/frenchbraid6.gif

Step 6: Take a section of hair from the left side of your head, and then add it to the strand that is on the left.

http://2good2lose.com/braids/frenchbraid7.gif

Step 7: Bring the left strand towards the middle, and then bring the middle strand over to the left. Make sure that your hands are close to your head, so that the strands could be held together tightly.

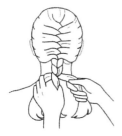

http://2good2lose.com/braids/frenchbraid8.gif

Step 8: Repeat steps 2 to 3 until you have used all your hair, and then finish with a basic braid. Fasten with an elastic.

Dutch Braid

http://www3.images.coolspotters.com/photos/851516/dutch-braid-profile.jpg

Step 1: Take a section of your hair, particularly from the crown area.

Step 2: Divide into three sections and start doing a regular braid. To make things as simple as possible, just call the sections Left, Right, and Middle.

Step 3: Braid for two cycles and when you have reached the third cycle, pull a section of your hair from the right side, and then combine this section with the right section of your hair. The trick is to go under instead of over. This differentiates it from a basic braid and from the French braid as well.

Step 4: Take a section of hair from the left side and braid it by letting the left section pass under the middle.

Step 5: Keep adding sections until you have reached the end of your hair. Tie with an elastic.

Chapter 2: Play with the Fishtail Braid

The Fishtail Braid is one of the most beautiful kinds of braids out there, and what's great about it is that you can create different fishtail braid styles depending on your mood or on the occasion. Learning how to do the fishtail braid would definitely be beneficial for you.

Basic Fishtail Braid

http://www.sofeminine.co.uk/beaute/how-to-hairstyles/fishtail-step-by-step.jpg

Step 1: Part your hair on the side, and then take its whole length to just one side.

Step 2: Split hair into two sections.

Step 3: Take a small section of hair from the outside section, and then bring that inside the opposite section.

Step 4: Then, take a section of hair again from outside the other section. This time though, bring the strand to the opposite section. Make sure that you pull it tight.

Step 5: Just continue taking sections from each side, putting them inside their opposite sections so that you would be able to create an inverted braid pattern.

Step 6: Continue doing so, until you have used all your hair.

Step 7: Tie with an elastic. You may also pull out some strands to give your fishtail braid a more natural, textured look.

Reverse Fishtail Braid

http://www.cutegirlshairstyles.com/wp-content/uploads/2013/05/IMG_1675.jpg

Step 1: Comb the hair into a high ponytail. You may also choose to just do it on the side, just like how you did the basic fishtail braid, and then secure it with an elastic band.

Step 2: Separate it into two equal sections.

Step 3: Take a portion of hair from the outside of the right section, and then take it behind the same section and combine it with the inside of the left section.

Step 4: Take another portion of hair from outside the left section. Take it behind the rest of the left section, and then combine it with the inside of the same section.

Step 5: Continue doing steps 3 and 4 until you have used all of your hair. Once you reach the end, secure it with an elastic and add a ribbon or strand of hair – tie things together to make them look sleeker.

Fluffy Fishtail Braid

http://www.cutegirlshairstyles.com/wp-content/uploads/2013/09/photo-2.jpg

Step 1: Tie hair into a high ponytail, and then take a small section of that hair and wrap it around an elastic. Secure with a bobby pin.

Step 2: Use a rat-tail comb (as seen above) to comb the back of your hair's top region. You can do this by lifting the layers of the hair and combing down to the roots. Make sure that you do this only to the part of your hair that is on top of the ponytail area.

Step 3: Gently brush the hair on the surface using a smoothing brush to remove any rough spots and for you to easily be able to tease your hair. Brushing, in that specific way, will make your hair straight and smooth.

Step 4: Now, move 6 to 8 inches down the ponytail and create a regular fishtail braid. After that, continue doing the braid, until you reach the last few inches near the ends. Secure everything together with an elastic.

Step 5: Lightly loosen the braid so that it will look more natural and fuller. It would also be best if you tug the hair on the section of the ponytail, for the sake of adding more volume. You may also choose to hold the braids in place by using hairspray.

Four-sided Fishtail Braid

http://www.cutegirlshairstyles.com/wp-content/uploads/2013/09/IMG_0539.jpg

Step 1: Brush hair and secure it into a regular ponytail using an elastic, and then divide it into two large strands.

Step 2: On the left side, take a section of hair from the outside edge. After doing that, cross it over to add it inside the right strand.

Step 3: Take a section of hair from the right area's outermost edge, and then cross it over to bring it inside the left strand. At this point, you have completed the first "full stitch" of the fishtail braid.

Step 4: Repeat steps 2 and 3, so that the second stitch of the fishtail braid would be complete.

Step 5: Take a small section of hair from the left's outside edge, and then cross it under that strand and add it inside the right section.

Step 6: Take a small section of hair from the right side's outside edge. Cross it under that strand, and then add it inside the left section.

Step 7: Repeat steps 5 and 6 to complete the second stitch of the reverse fishtail braid.

Step 8: Repeat steps 2 to 7 by alternating between regular fishtail stitches and two reverse fishtail stitches. Continue until you run out of hair to braid.

Step 9: Secure the end of the braid with an elastic. You may hide the elastic using a strand of hair or some bobby pins. Using flower pins instead should create a dainty effect.

Twisted Double Fishtail

http://www.cutegirlshairstyles.com/wp-content/uploads/2013/12/IMG_2723.jpg

Step 1: Sweep all your hair to one side, and then separate the hair into two smaller sections. Don't mind one of the sections for now.

Step 2: Create a regular fishtail braid on the free section.

Step 3: After creating a fishtail braid, secure it with an elastic and create another fishtail braid using the other strand of hair – the one that you have disregarded earlier.

Step 4: After finishing the other fishtail braid, secure it with an elastic as well.

Step 5: Take the two finished fishtail braids and wrap them around each other to create a fishtail twist effect.

Step 6: Remove the elastics that you have used earlier and secure both braids using another elastic band. Use bobby pins to hide the elastic.

Ponytail with Fishtail Accents

http://www.cutegirlshairstyles.com/wp-content/uploads/2014/03/N0A0830.jpg

Step 1: Create a square section, using hair that can be found at the top of the head.

Step 2: Create a pompadour, and then tease it a bit to add volume underneath. Smooth the top using a smoothing brush (as pictured below).

http://s1.folica.com/img/product/0/005597/main-view/cricket-smoothing-brush-278x278.jpg

Step 3: Secure this section using an elastic. It would be best to use one that matches your hair color. Clip the braid (that one you've just worked on) out of the way for the meantime.

Step 4: Create a fishtail braid on this section, and then secure it using another elastic band that matches your hair color. Clip the braid out of the way again.

Step 5: Pull the rest of your hair back to the base of your neck, and then tie your hair with an elastic or a ponytail holder.

Step 6: Take a light of hair from the ponytail, and then wrap it around the ponytail using an elastic. As usual, you'll need to hide the elastic with bobby pins.

Step 7: Unclip the fishtail and place it straight down the head, directly over the wrapped section.

Step 8: Use bobby pins to secure the fishtail against your head, on the spot where you have secured the ponytail earlier. Add hairspray or accessories if necessary.

Fishtail Braid with Yarn Extension

http://www.cutegirlshairstyles.com/wp-content/uploads/2013/04/IMG_1558.jpg

Step 1: Section off the top part of the hair by securing it using a rubber band. Keep it out of the way for a bit.

Step 2: Get one strand of yarn and tie it on the base of the strand of hair that is hanging. This can be done by putting the yarn perpendicular to the hair, then tying a simple knot (using the yarn) around it. Tease the hair to keep the knot from slipping.

Step 3: Grab another piece of yarn, but this time, in a different color. Tie it to the next strand of your hair.

Step 4: Upon using all the strands of yarn that you have, you should move down the remaining sections your hair (particularly those on your head's topmost region) so that you can hide the knots.

Step 5: Sweep all your hair towards one shoulder. Separate your hair into two sections afterwards.

Step 6: Create a regular fishtail braid using a small section of your hair. Cross it over and into the other section, and be sure to "inject" a piece of yarn while doing so.

Step 7: Repeat step 6 on the other side.

Step 8: Repeat steps 6 and 7 until you reach the end of your hair, and do make sure to add a piece of yarn per stitch.

Step 9: Secure the fishtail braid with an elastic.

Fishtail Bun

http://www.oncewed.com/wp-content/uploads/2012/11/wedding-hairstyles-updos-tutorial-diy2.jpg

Step 1: Use any kind of product that effectively (and conveniently) adds volume to your hair. Then, curl your hair up a bit. Backcomb or tease it to form some sort of crown, and then proceed to do a fishtail braid.

Step 2: Pull the braid so that it would be a bit loose and look natural.

Step 3: Twist the braid into a bun and secure with bobby pins.

Chapter 3: Braids for Weddings and Parties

Now, if you are feeling more creative and want to try other varieties of braids that you can wear during events, such as parties, weddings, or other social gatherings, feel free to do so. In this chapter, you will learn how to create these so-called "more complex" kinds of braids that will surely leave your friends in awe.

Waterfall Braids

http://hellogiggles.hellogiggles.netdna-cdn.com/wp-content/uploads/2013/06/13/Waterfall3-e1371157817568-320x480.jpg

Step 1: Pick three sections of your hair and begin to French braid them.

Step 2: Upon crossing the top section of your hair over, let go of the piece of hair that you have used so that it will be left hanging.

Step 3: Pick up another section of hair in order to replace the hair that's hanging.

Step 4: Continue steps 2 and 3. Keep on doing a French braid until you have used all of your hair.

Mermaid Tail Braid

http://2.bp.blogspot.com/-yQavG5g4U4E/T6hvHBgnwlI/AAAAAAAA03Y/G7elwrnoFKo/s1600/hair-tutorial-mermaid-braid.jpg

Step 1: Divide hair into two equal sections.

Step 2: Braid each section of your hair, and then tie each section with an elastic band. After doing that, create a Dutch Braid (if you've already forgotten how to make one, reread the first chapter).

Step 3: Fatten the braids by pulling the outer edges out carefully.

Step 4: Line up the two braided sections so that they will look like one big braid. You should be cautious with the middle part (between the braids), as you have to make sure that it lines up the braids properly. By doing that, you'll have braids that look really natural.

Step 5: Pin the middle part of the two braids to make sure that they are held together tightly, and then secure the braids with elastics.

Bohemian Braid

Step 1: Part your hair, moving it towards one side of your head.

Step 2: Divide the hair into two sections (along the parted area), with one section just near the forehead and the other directly behind it.

Step 3: Twist the sections so that the one at the back will now be in front.

Step 4: Add more hair by taking some from your hairline, and then angle the braid along one side of your face. Once you're done, twist the two sections once more.

http://pad3.whstatic.com/images/thumb/8/8c/Braid-Your-Hair-for-Weddings-Step-2Bullet5.jpg/670px-Braid-Your-Hair-for-Weddings-Step-2Bullet5.jpg

Step 5: Secure the braids with hair elastic and put bobby pins just behind your ear, then style it the way you want.

http://pad2.whstatic.com/images/thumb/2/28/Braid-Your-Hair-for-Weddings-Step-2.jpg/670px-Braid-Your-Hair-for-Weddings-Step-2.jpg

Five Braid Up-do

http://www.makeupgeek.com/wp-content/uploads/2012/07/Braided-updo-02-550x462.jpg

Step 1: It would be good to curl your hair first before proceeding with this Up-do, as doing so would make the hair look more natural and voluminous. In other words, it'd be much better than a mere "messy up-do."

Step 2: Part the hair into five sections, and then start braiding each. Once you're done, secure the braids with elastics.

Step 3: Lightly pull the sides of your hair to give it more volume.

http://www.makeupgeek.com/wp-content/uploads/2012/07/Braided-Updo-5-550x432.jpg

Step 4: Take one of the sections at the bottom, and then cross it over the opposite side with some bobby pins.

http://www.makeupgeek.com/wp-content/uploads/2012/07/Braided-Updo-7-550x491.jpg

Step 5: Do the same thing with the braids on the opposite side, so that the braids would now overlap one another.

Step 6: Take the very bottom part of the braid, and then wrap it around the rest of the other braids. Secure with bobby pins.

http://www.makeupgeek.com/wp-content/uploads/2012/07/Braided-updo-9-511x750.jpg

Step 7: Take the braids from the front, and then cover the loose ends with bobby pins. Overlap the braids and add hairspray so that the up-do will be held tightly.

Pretzel Braid

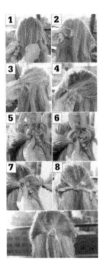

http://www.seventeen.com/cm/seventeen/images/rF/sev-pretzel-braid-tutorial-blog.jpg

Step 1: Take an inch of hair from behind each of your temples. It would be easier to proceed with the rest of the instructions if your hair is wet (or at the very least, damp), so spray on some water before doing so.

Step 2: Loop the left strand of the hair and hold it with your thumb and your first two fingers.

Step 3: Pull the other strand over the top section, where the loop crosses.

Step 4: Reach between the two sections of hair, and then loop the second strand up and under the first strand, until it reaches the left side where the loop crosses.

Step 5: Cross the top half of the first loop, and then cross the end of the second loop under its other half.

Step 6: Pull the second strand over the bottom loop of the first strand.

Step 7: Tug at both of the loose ends in order to finish the knot.

Chapter 4: Braids in the Media

As mentioned earlier, braids have become quite popular – not only because of their beauty, but also because there are some movies and TV shows with characters who are known for their braids. That's why their fans tend to follow their hairstyles by hiring hairdressers. That's also why more and more are trying to learn how to do those popular braids. Now, you have the chance to learn how to do the braids of some popular movie and television-show characters. Here are some good examples.

Katniss Everdeen (Hunger Games) Braids

http://fashioncouchdotcom.files.wordpress.com/2012/03/katniss.png

http://www.makeupgeek.com/wp-content/uploads/2012/03/021-550x366.jpg

Step 1: Take a section of your hair, and then split it into three smaller sections.

http://www.makeupgeek.com/wp-content/uploads/2012/03/03-500x750.jpg

Step 2: Take the first section and pull it under the second section, then take the third section and bring it under the first section.

http://www.makeupgeek.com/wp-content/uploads/2012/03/06-500x750.jpg

Step 3: Add hair into the second section, and then hold the second section and bring it under the third section.

Step 4: Add hair to the first section and hold it between your fingers. Afterwards, bring the said part of your hair under the braid.

Step 5: Continue adding more hair, and then pull the braids under the group of hair. Do the same to those over it. It's like doing a reverse French Braid.

http://www.makeupgeek.com/wp-content/uploads/2012/03/09-550x366.jpg

Step 6: Continue braiding all the way down.

http://www.makeupgeek.com/wp-content/uploads/2012/03/102-519x750.jpg\

Step 7: Pull the hair tightly so that it stays in place. There you have it, your very own Katniss Everdeen braids!

http://www.makeupgeek.com/wp-content/uploads/2012/03/1310-550x418.jpg

Primrose Everdeen (Hunger Games) Braids

http://img1.wikia.nocookie.net/__cb20120214014728/thehungergames/images/9/9d/Primrose_Everdeen_12.jpg

http://zelocare.files.wordpress.com/2013/10/catching-fire-braid-top-arrows.jpg?w=584&h=438

Step 1: Make a side-part, and then divide your hair into two sections.

Step 2: Make an inverted braid at the end of the side-part, near the forehead, while grasping additional hair from the forehead line. After doing that, move the braid down and around.

Step 3: Continue braiding across the back of your head while grasping additional strands of hair from the side nearest your head, until you get to reach your other ear. Move down towards the length of the hair, and then secure the ends with an elastic or a hair tie.

http://zelocare.files.wordpress.com/2013/10/20130912_142354.jpg?w=584&h=778

Princess Leia (Star Wars) Braids

http://i2.wp.com/rebelshaven.com/images/leia/leia033.jpg?resize=300%2C365

Step 1: Brush your hair and tie it into a low ponytail. Once you're done, divide it into three sections. Note that the middle section should be thicker than the other sections.

Step 2: Braid each section. Doing the basic braiding technique is fine, so just continue braiding all the way down.

http://i1.wp.com/www.whitehotroom.com/wp-content/uploads/diy_leia05.jpg?resize=350%2C232

Step 3: Wrap the left and right braids around your head and make sure that the ends overlap. Secure with hairspray and bobby pins.

Step 4: Wrap the thick braid around the ponytail holder, and then tuck the ends beneath. Secure everything together with bobby pins.

http://i1.wp.com/www.whitehotroom.com/wp-content/uploads/diy_leia08.jpg?resize=350%2C232

Khaleesi/Daenerys (The Game of Thrones) Hairstyle

http://www.moneyaftergraduation.com/wp-content/uploads/2013/07/khaleesi-braids.jpg

Step 1: French braid your hair. Go to sleep without undoing it.

Step 2: The following day, take out the braids. At this point, your hair should be very wavy.

Step 3: Part your hair in the middle, and then select a 2- to 3-inch section. Begin doing a Dutch braid afterwards.

Step 4: Braid towards the back of your crown, but do not pick up extra hair (don't mind those strands lying around). Braid to the ends, and then secure everything together with elastics.

http://www.moneyaftergraduation.com/wp-content/uploads/2013/07/Photo-on-2013-07-13-at-12.31-PM.jpg

Step 5: Loosen your braids a bit, so they could have more volume.

http://www.moneyaftergraduation.com/wp-content/uploads/2013/07/Photo-on-2013-07-13-at-12.33-PM.jpg

Step 6: Repeat the Process on the other part of your hair.

Step 7: Pin both braids to the back of your hair and leave them there for a bit.

Step 8: Start braiding the lower part of your hair and add strands of your hair to the braid (as shown below). Repeat process on the other side of your hair as well.

http://www.moneyaftergraduation.com/wp-content/uploads/2013/07/Photo-on-2013-07-13-at-12.43-PM.jpg

Step 9: Get the two braided strands that you have pinned back earlier and combine them. To do this, you have to hold them together using an elastic tie, and then undo the braids while holding them together with an elastic. Take the elastic band out, then combine the outside and middle parts of the braids into a single strand. Afterwards, take the two strands together to make them as one.

http://www.moneyaftergraduation.com/wp-content/uploads/2013/07/Photo-on-2013-07-13-at-12.53-PM.jpg

Step 10: Combine the lower two braids, and then twist the combined braids around the lower braid to achieve full "Khaleesi effect."

http://www.moneyaftergraduation.com/wp-content/uploads/2013/07/IMG_3256-768x1024.jpg

Sansa Stark (The Game of Thrones) Braids

http://www.moneyaftergraduation.com/wp-content/uploads/2013/07/Joffrey-Sansa-game-of-thrones-21989762-1920-1080.jpg

Step 1: French braid your hair, and then sleep with it on. Take it out the following day, so you could have your own set of waves.

Step 2: Cross over the braid to the other side of the hair. Make sure that you take the outside part first as that is how Sansa's braid is made.

Step 3: Braid back towards your crown. Pull the hair tightly so that the braids would stick together. The hair you have pulled from the braid should now lie on the top of your head, and the hair you've pulled into the braid should now be under your head.

http://www.moneyaftergraduation.com/wp-content/uploads/2013/07/Photo-on-2013-07-13-at-11.38-AM-2.jpg

Step 4: End the French braid once you have reached your crown, and then move on to do the basic braid towards the end of your hair. Repeat this process on the other side of the hair.

http://www.moneyaftergraduation.com/wp-content/uploads/2013/07/Photo-on-2013-07-13-at-11.40-AM-3.jpg

Step 5: When both of the braids are complete, twist them together and secure with an elastic tie.

http://www.moneyaftergraduation.com/wp-content/uploads/2013/07/Photo-on-2013-07-13-at-11.55-AM.jpg

Step 6: Remove the elastic ties that are holding the small braid, and then unravel them towards the elastics that are holding the other braids together. At this point, you're already wearing Sansa Stark's hairstyle!

Chapter 5: Other Kinds of Braids

There are braids that you can make without paying too much attention to the question of "Why?" Whether you're going to attend a special gathering or you just feel like having a new hairstyle, you could choose among the many braids in this chapter. These braids will surely get the attention of your family and friends, and will surely make you feel better about yourself.

The Romantic Rosette

Step 1: Pull your hair back, and then secure it with a rubber band or an elastic tie.

Step 2: Divide your hair into three sections. Braid each of those sections.

http://artzycreations.com/wp-content/uploads/2013/11/Three-Braids1.jpg

Step 3: Take each section of your hair and wrap them in a circle. Tuck the ends underneath, and then pin the "rosettes" or the circles. That's it, that's how easy it is to create Romantic Rosette Braids that will surely make you the talk of the town!

http://artzycreations.com/wp-content/uploads/2013/11/Final-Image-copy.jpg

The Double Braid

http://4.bp.blogspot.com/-QmZzxP5mlXk/UAZAbtzzAVI/AAAAAAAAD0Y/iUVrrqB-yp0/s1600/double+braid+hair+tutorial.jpg

Step 1: Put your hair down, and then take a thick section of your hair and braid it all the way down.

Step 2: The braid should now lie flat on your head. Tug the braid slightly, be careful not to let it totally unravel, so that it will look "thicker".

Step 3: After finishing the braid, pin it back on the side of your head.

Step 4: Now, you should begin braiding the rest of your hair into a side-braid and do not forget to tug every once in a while to make your hair look "fuller." Use a bit of hairspray if you want to keep the braids in place for much longer.

The Brisk Braid

Step 1: Tie your hair into a low ponytail, and then gently pull at it for that extra boost in volume.

Step 2: Braid your hair in the loosened ponytail.

http://2.bp.blogspot.com/-oInZURr-
zXo/UCGjt21kb3I/AAAAAAAAEEs/_026zF9yXYk/s1600/The+Brisk+Braid+Wrap+Tutorial.jpg

Step 3: Create what seems like a "hole" in the middle of your hair, right where you have tied it, and then pull the braid through the said hole.

http://2.bp.blogspot.com/-oInZURr-
zXo/UCGjt21kb3I/AAAAAAAAEEs/_026zF9yXYk/s1600/The+Brisk+Braid+Wrap+Tutorial.jpg

Step 4: Repeat the previous step so that the braid could be spread out. This is an important thing to do, as it helps your hair maintain its volume and thickness.

Step 5: Tuck the end of the braid and secure it with bobby pins. You may also use hairspray, as doing so makes your braids a lot stronger, preventing them from unraveling by themselves.

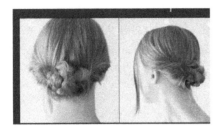

http://2.bp.blogspot.com/-0InZURr-
zX0/UCGjt21kb3I/AAAAAAAAEEs/_026zF9yXYk/s1600/The+Brisk+Braid+Wrap+Tutorial.jpg

The Half Crown Braid

http://www.hairromance.com/wp-content/uploads/2013/04/Hair-Romance-hairstyle-tutorial-half-crown-braid.jpg

Step 1: Take 1- to 2-inch sections of your hair from one side of your head, just above your ear. Split this section into three parts, and then create a braid.

Step 2: Angle the braid at the back of your head, going around the head. Secure the braid with an elastic.

Step 3: Repeat the process on the other side of your head. Make a plait and secure the end with an elastic band.

Step 4: Put the braid at the back of your head, use bobby pins to keep the braid in place.

Step 5: Cross the second strand of hair over the first, and then tuck it behind the first braided hair. Secure everything together with bobby pins.

Double Pigtail Braid

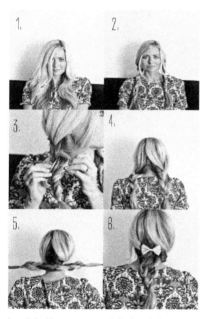

http://1.bp.blogspot.com/-7-cDbvfv9ds/Uci9LjS_-6I/AAAAAAAAHRk/UolLHljMDOo/s1600/Recently+Updated8+copy.jpg

Step 1: Part down the middle of your hair.

Step 2: Make two pigtail braids and secure them at each end with elastics.

Step 3: Pull up the braid strands so that you can loosen them up, and then proceed to make a thicker braid.

Step 4: Repeat the process on the other side of your hair, and then bring your hair to the back.

Step 5: Twist your pigtails together, moving them to the other side of your hair.

Step 6: Take out one of the elastics that you have used earlier, and then use it to secure the pigtail braids together (twist the pigtails together first though). You can use a bow, a ribbon, or a flower tie to hide the elastics and make the braids look a lot better.

Boho Rose Braid

http://4.bp.blogspot.com/-U2tF5W7mSIU/UWLQOJ7njdI/AAAAAAAANC4/PmIx8YtAMJI/s1600/boho+rose+braid.jpg

Step 1: Take a medium to large section of your hair that's close to your right ear.

Step 2: Braid the said section from front to back.

Step 3: Repeat on the opposite side of your head.

Step 4: Bring both of the braids to your back, and then secure them with elastic bands.

Step 5: Loosen the braids, and then pull them gently with your fingers.

Step 6: Take one of the braids and wrap it upon itself to create a small braided bun.

Step 7: Secure the ends with bobby pins. Add hair accessories if you prefer.

Conclusion

Thank you for downloading this book!

I hope this book was able to help you learn about the different kinds of braids. Hopefully, you've also learned how to create them yourself. Who knows? After doing the braids for yourself, maybe you can also try doing them on others. When you become skilled enough, maybe you could even earn an extra from your braiding endeavors.

Braids are fun and beautiful, and now, you have the chance to create different kinds of braids. After all, you've learned about the most popular ones by reading this book. It's best to tell you though, that there are many other types of braids left for you to discover. So, don't stop learning.

Finally, if you enjoyed this book, please post a review on Amazon. It would not take much of your time and it will be greatly appreciated.

Thank you and good luck!

Chapter 5: Basic Instructions for Beginner Quilters

It's a good thing that more and more people are becoming hooked with quilted items, which inspires them to learn how to do quilting. Listed below are some basic instructions which may serve as excellent guidelines for aspiring quilters. The instructions may as well serve as a little refresher course for those who have already tried quilting before.

Before the Sewing Process...

There is no doubt that making a quilt is very exciting, whether it is the person's initial quilt or his 50th quilt. It is important to thoroughly read and comprehend the pattern instructions before the aspiring quilter start the cutting process. It is also relevant to choose a high quality 100% cotton fabric.

Majority of those who love to do quilting opt to prewash their chosen fabric prior to sewing in order to make sure that bleeding of dyes or shrinkage will be avoided before the material is processed into a quilt, especially if the end result will be used and washed regularly. The quality of the fabrics and the dyes used in quilting has enhanced greatly, however, there are still some quilters who ignore this important step.

Cutting the Chosen Fabric Using a Rotary Cutter

Majority of quilters at present utilize a cutting mat and rotary cutter in cutting the fabric that will be quilted, though there is a possibility to create explicit and precise quilts by utilizing templates. The following instructions involved the different rotary cutting technique, since it is the most used methodology.

Each and every strip is cut in accordance to the fabric's width, unless otherwise stated. The beginner quilter should cut the chosen material in half lengthwise, the selvedges must be together, ensuring that the fabric lies unwrinkled and smooth. The Fold again in half in order for the edge of the selvedge to meet the fold.

Place a marked line on the ruler particularly on the fabric folded edge. Utilize a rotary cutter in cutting a straight edge, specifically on the fabric's right-hand edge.

If the quilter is right-handed, he should turn his cutting mat around (take note that the mat is the one that will be moved and not the fabric), so that he can cut strips coming from the fabric's left side. If the quilter is left handed, he should cut strips coming from the fabric's right side, to leave the fabric and mat as is.

Aspiring quilters should ensure that they'll cut their preferred fabrics away from their selves and not towards them. Also, when not in use, the rotary cutter must not be exposed to avoid accidents. Take note that this cutter's blade is indeed sharp.

Referring to the chosen quilt pattern, the quilter should cut strips in accordance to the needed width and then he should cut strips that are required to make quilt pieces, such as triangles, rectangles, squares and a lot more. To ensure the evenness of the cut edges, the quilter should move the ruler (not the chosen fabric).

Check after making 3 to 4 strips to ensure that they're straight. If it's necessary, trim the fabric once more. Excellent cutting facilitates good piecing and quilting.

Cutting with Templates, Cutting for Applique

Templates that have quilt pattern are typically available in full size. If the templates require a seam allowance of ¼, the best stitching line is dashed line and the ideal solid line is cutting line. Aspiring quilters must remember that the templates intended for hand piecing don't need seam allowance, while the templates intended for machine piecing require seam allowance.

Different Applique Techniques

The applique can be placed to the quilt either by hand or by using a machine. There are actually 3 kinds of Applique techniques and these are:

Machine Applique. The method of preparation of applique pieces that are for machine stitching is referred to as freezer paper and starch technique. Those applique shapes that don't have seam allowance must be craft using freezer paper. The quilter must press the freezer paper's shiny side to the fabric's wrong side and then, cut around the template. The quilter should leave approximately ¼" seam allowance.

Pour or spray liquid starch in a small container. Using a tiny paint brush or Q-tip, the seam allowance that surrounds the freezer paper template must be painted with starch. After which, by utilizing an iron, the quilter should press the seam allowance on top of the freezer paper template, the quilter should make the template as his guide. If there's a need to clip the curves then do so.

Usually, the outside curves don't have to be clipped, since the fabric will eventually stretch for those. The inside curves on the other hand can be clipped, however, the quilter must ensure that the clipping will enable the extra material to be eased in. To accomplish this task, the quilter may utilize a craft iron, though this can as well be done using a regular-sized iron.

The quilter may utilize a metal or wooden skewer in holding down the fabric while pressing. No matter how the applique's underside looks like, the quilter must ensure that the right side is smooth and flat. The pressed and folded edge must as well be flat and smooth. Once the pieces cooled down, the quilter can thoroughly take off the freezer paper.

Place the appliques on the background fabric and then pin or glue it so that it will stay on place. Today, there are variations of glues that can be utilized in appliqueing. By utilizing a blind hemstitch, decorative stitch, blanket stitch, satin stitch, or straight stitch, the quilter must machine stitch around every applique. If the quilter doesn't want to make his stitching obvious, he can blind his preferred stitching technique using a monofilament thread.

Fusible Web Applique. Whenever the quilter is using a fusible web, he should always follow the instructions of the manufacturer. Take not that there's a possibility that the instructions of a certain manufacturer is different from other manufacturers. Asymmetrical pieces are required to be flipped, but if the quilt pattern has mirror image template, then there's no need to do so. The quilter should trace the appliques. On the fusible web's paper side.

The quilter should cut shapes out roughly and then fuse these shapes to the fabric's wrong side.

The quilter should take off the paper backing and then fuse his applique to his background fabric.

The quilter may utilize a satin stitch, blanket stitch or any kind of decorative stitch to hold his appliques in place. If the quilter wants to have a raw edge appearance, he can simply use the straight stitch when stitching the surrounding edges of his applique.

Needle-Turn Applique. The quilter should trace the applique pieces on the fabric's right side, adding a seam allowance of mere ¼" that is if it is not included on the template. The door should pin applique on the fabric's background and then stitch it in place. He should start with the underneath pieces. The quilter should utilize his needle to shift the seam allowance beneath as he stitches and utilizes a thread. The stitches must be placed approximately 1/8 inches to ¼ inches apart.

This particular technique needs sufficient practice in order to make the stitches nearly invisible and even. However, there are a lot of quilters who find this technique relaxing. Also, they love the fact that this is a portable project, thus, they can do this while travelling.

Tips in Piecing

The quilter should utilize a fairly short length stitch, approximately 12 stitches or 2.5 mm to the inch. Each and every seam allowance utilized in quilting are ¼ inches, unless it is stated. The quilter should mark the throat plate using a tape, about ¼" going to the right of the location of the needle pierces to be accurate.

When sewing together many similar fragments, the quilter can chain stitch. This simply means that the quilter should not stop and then cut the thread at the seam's end. Instead, the quilter must feed the next pieces under his foot and then continue sewing. Once the piecing is done, he should go back and then cut the threads that are in between every set of pieces. He must ensure that he will always trim off thread tails at the start and end of every seam.

Tips for Pressing

Press using an iron. A hot iron is needed to even out flat and crisp seams. When pressing, initially press on the stitching line in order to set the seam. The next thing to do is press the seam on one of its side, typically on the darker fabric. Adjoining seams are required to be pressed or ironed in opposite directions. The secret to accomplish this task is follow the pattern, especially if there are special instructions.

When Adding Borders

The quilter have to measure the middle of the top part of the quilt at few areas lengthwise and then utilize the average of the acquired measurements as the side border measurements. The quilter must pin and sew the 2-side borders, easing the top of the quilt to fit, and then sew along with a ¼" seam.

The quilter must press the seam to the border. He should as well measure through the middle of the quilt along with adhered side borders widthwise in certain spots in the quilt and utilize the average of the measurements for the top border and bottom border, and then sew in place.

The Quilt Sandwich

The batting and the back o the quilt must be cut about 3 inches bigger on all sides, bigger than the top part of the quilt. Cut every selvedge off any edges or seams. Put the quilt back on a smooth and flat surface, the wrong side up.

Put a layer of batting (similar size as with the batting).

Center of the top part of the quilt on backing and batting.

The quilter need to hold the 3 layers temporarily. He may opt to hand-baste it by utilizing big running stitches, basting about 4 inches apart in every direction. The quilter can pin the sandwich together using safety pins. He may as well opt to utilize a temporary spray adhesive on every layer. This is efficient on a tiny quilt.

When quilting using a machine, according to professional quilters, the best method to utilize is "Stitch in the Ditch". This pertains to stitching a straight line along the seams. The quilter should take time and he should guide the guilt without pulling or pushing.

If you enjoy this preview, then _click here for the full story of this eBook!_

Or go to: _http://www.amazon.com/dp/B00J3UM59W/_

Kindly Check My Other Works!

Hereunder, you will find a few of my eBooks that presently live at Amazon. Just click the following Title Links to check them out, to wit;

- _Amazon Affiliate: The Ultimate Guide to Making Money on Amazon_

- _Facebook Marketing – The Ultimate Guide to Marketing Facebook_

- _How to Train your Dog: The Ultimate Step by Step Guide_

- _How to Write a Screenplay – Screenwriting Made Easy_

- _The Texting Game for Guys: Proven Clear Cut Methods to Creating Attraction through Texting Today_

- _The Best of Les Brown: Learn the Life Changing Principles of Success Today_

If the links do not work for whatever reasons, simply search for those titles on the Amazon to find them.

Other free eBooks are now available, _click here for your subscription!_

CPSIA information can be obtained
at www.ICGtesting.com
Printed in the USA
LVHW080749210620
PP15965500001B/10